JANE LONG

CHOOSING TEXAS

MARY DODSON WADE

ILLUSTRATIONS BY

VIRGINIA MARSH ROEDER

NOT AFRAID

Jane Long was called the "Mother of Texas." She came to Texas before almost any other Americans.

Bad things sometimes happened to her. But she did not give up. She lived a long, busy life.

LEAVING FOR MISSISSIPPI

Jane Herbert Wilkinson was born in Maryland on July 23, 1798. She was the youngest of ten children.

Jane's father died the year after she was born. Twelve years later, Jane's mother moved the family to Mississippi. The next year her mother died. Jane stayed in Mississippi with her sister, Barbara.

CHOOSING A HUSBAND

When Jane was sixteen, Dr. James Long visited their house. He and Jane fell in love. Two weeks later they married. The next year little Ann was born.

James Long wanted Texas to be part of the United States. But Texas belonged to Spain. James Long led soldiers to Texas. They carried a red and white flag Jane and her sister had made.

Jane stayed home. A few weeks later, little Rebecca was born.
Jane left her children with her sister and hurried to her husband.

Spanish soldiers came. They chased the Americans back home.
Sad news greeted the Longs. Their baby had died.

DINNER WITH A PIRATE

James Long went back to Texas. Jane went too. She took Ann and her slave, Kian, with her.

The soldiers built a mud fort at Bolivar Point. Pirate Jean Lafitte lived nearby on Galveston Island.

The pirate invited the Longs for dinner on his ship. Jane was surprised. He had nice manners and served food on elegant dishes.

ALONE

James Long marched off to capture more of Texas. He told Jane that he would be back soon.

Weeks went by. Everyone left. Jane would not go with them. "I will wait for my husband," she said.

Jane, Ann, and Kian were alone. They fished for food. They did not want the Indians to know that the soldiers were gone. She and Kian put a red dress on the flag pole. They fired the cannon.

Ice covered everything that winter. During a storm, baby Mary James was born.

Then spring came. Ships arrived. They gave the starving family food.

LAND FOR WIDOW

Finally, Jane heard sad news. James Long was dead. She was a widow. Before long, her baby died too.

Jane was nearly 30 years old. Stephen Austin had brought settlers to Texas. Jane, Ann, and Kian went to his colony on the Brazos River.

Stephen Austin gave Jane land. She pulled grass and threw rocks to show that she owned the land.

FEEDING IMPORTANT MEN

Jane did not build on her land right away. First, she went to Brazoria. Kian helped her run a boarding house.

People came to her boarding house to sleep and eat. Many important people like Sam Houston, William Travis, Ben Milam, and Mirabeau Lamar were her guests.

Stephen Austin was put in jail in Mexico City.

When he got home, a big party was held at Jane's boarding house. She and Kian set the tables three times to feed everybody. People danced until dawn.

SUCCESS

A man bought some of Jane's land. He built the town of Richmond. Jane opened a boarding house there.

After a few years, Jane moved to her land on the Brazos. She built a house and farmed.

Slaves picked her cotton. She raised cattle. Her brand was her initials. Jane became one of the richest people in Texas.

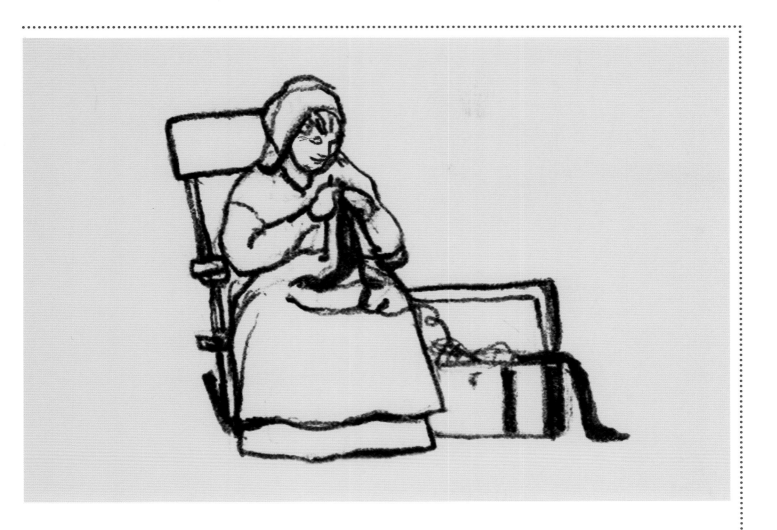

LIVING IN RICHMOND

Jane never married again. She often told the story of her life.
Her friend, Mirabeau Lamar, wrote it down.

When she grew old, Jane went to live with her grandson. "Aunt
Jane" walked around Richmond with a pipe in her mouth.

EATING ICE CREAM

She was 82 years old. A new Kian now took care of her. Young Kian was the granddaughter of the one who came to Texas with Jane.

Jane did not take walks any more. One day, she and Kian went for a ride around Richmond. They stopped and ate ice cream.

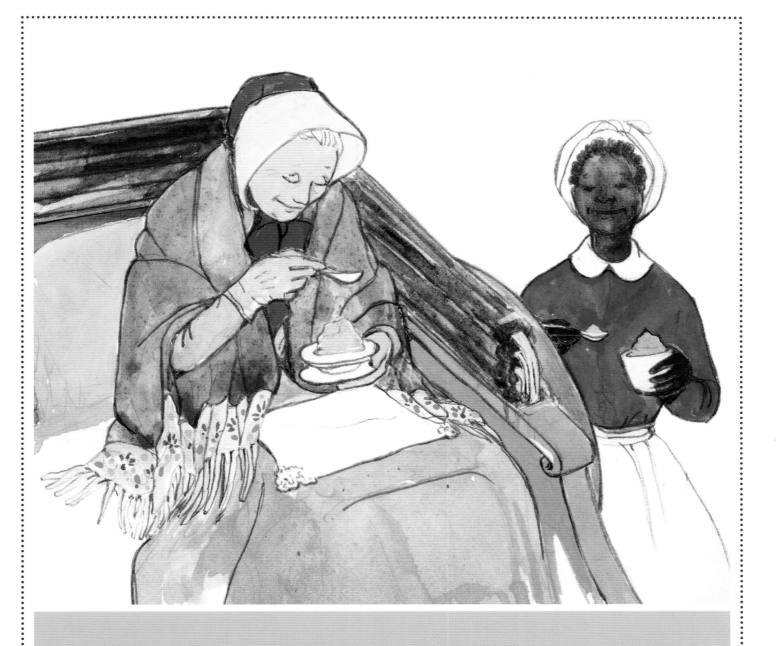

A month later, on December 30, 1880, Jane Long died.

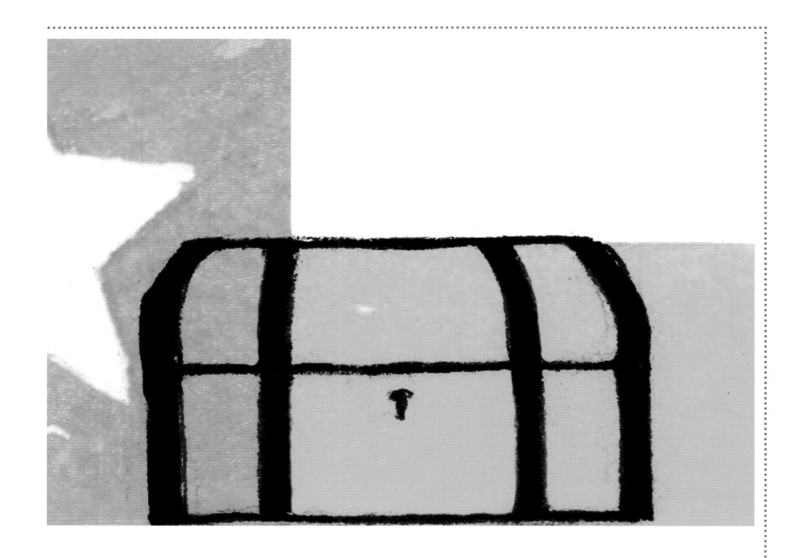

IT HAPPENED LATER

Jane Herbert Wilkinson Long is buried in Morton Cemetery in Richmond, Texas. During the Texas Centennial in 1836, a monument was placed on her grave.

The Fort Bend County Museum in Richmond has Jane Long's portrait and her piano.

**Jane Herbert Long's
cattle brand**

MARY DODSON WADE, a former educator and librarian, is the author of
more than fifty books for children, including *Christopher Columbus, Cinco de Mayo,
I Am Houston, I'm Going to Texas/Yo Voy a Tejas, President's Day,
C.S. Lewis: The Chronicler of Narnia* and *Joan Lowery Nixon: Masterful Mystery Writer*.
She and her husband live in Houston, Texas, and enjoy traveling.

VIRGINIA MARSH ROEDER taught Art at St. John's School in Houston Texas
for many years. She is the illustrator of many books for children, including
Phoebe Clapsaddle and the *Tumbleweed Gang*. She lives in Houston.

Look for more **Texas Heroes for Young Readers**
from Bright Sky Press:

Stephen F. Austin: Keeping Promises
David Crockett: Creating a Legend
Sam Houston: Standing Firm